ather

Nicola Tuxworth

Sunshine

When the Sun shines,
it is warm and bright.

blazing, yellow Sun

It is dry and hot in
the sunny desert.

Flowers
need sunshine
to grow.

Don't forget the suncream!

A chilly ice lolly is nice in hot weather.

A dip in the pool will keep you cool!

Clouds

There are lots of different kinds of cloud.

rumbling, storm clouds

grey, rain clouds

red clouds at sunset

small, fluffy clouds

What shapes have you
seen in the clouds?

Rain

Water that falls from clouds is called rain.

lashing rain

gentle raindrops

Plants need rain to grow.

Has it stopped
raining yet?

Do you like playing
in the rain?

Snow and ice

When the air is very cold, snowflakes fall from the clouds.

frosty icicles

Thick snow looks like a white blanket.

glistening snowflake

Wheee!
Tobogganing
is fun!

big, friendly
snowman

Thick
clothes
keep the
cold out.

Fog and mist

Cloud that is near to the ground is called fog.

When it is foggy at sea, a lighthouse warns ships about the coastline.

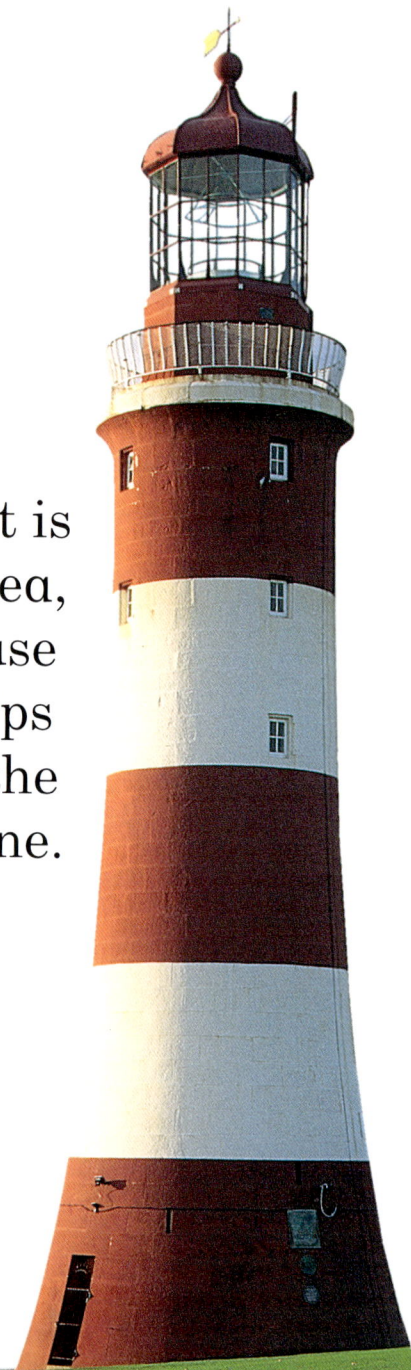

Why do you think fog is dangerous for drivers?

Mist is not as thick as fog. It is often misty before the Sun rises.

misty morning

What can you see through the mist?

Wind and storms

It is windy when the air about us moves.

Wind can blow your umbrella inside-out...

Can you feel the wind on your face?

...and turn a windmill's sails round.

In a storm you
might see flashes
of lightning...

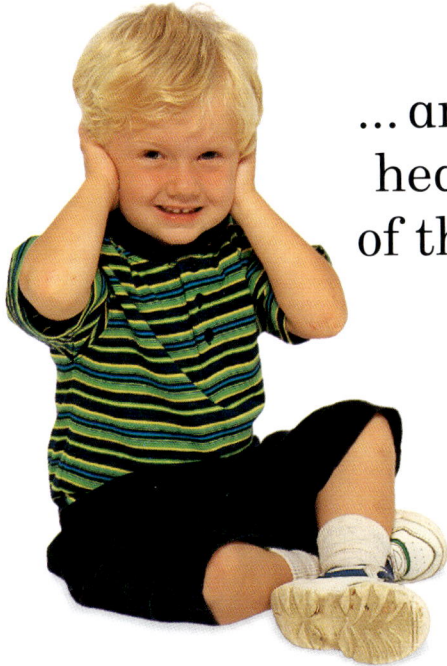

...and then
hear claps
of thunder.

What do you
think has
happened to
this tree?

People and weather

Weather is fun to play in, and it is important, too.

Have you ever been on a hot, sunny beach...

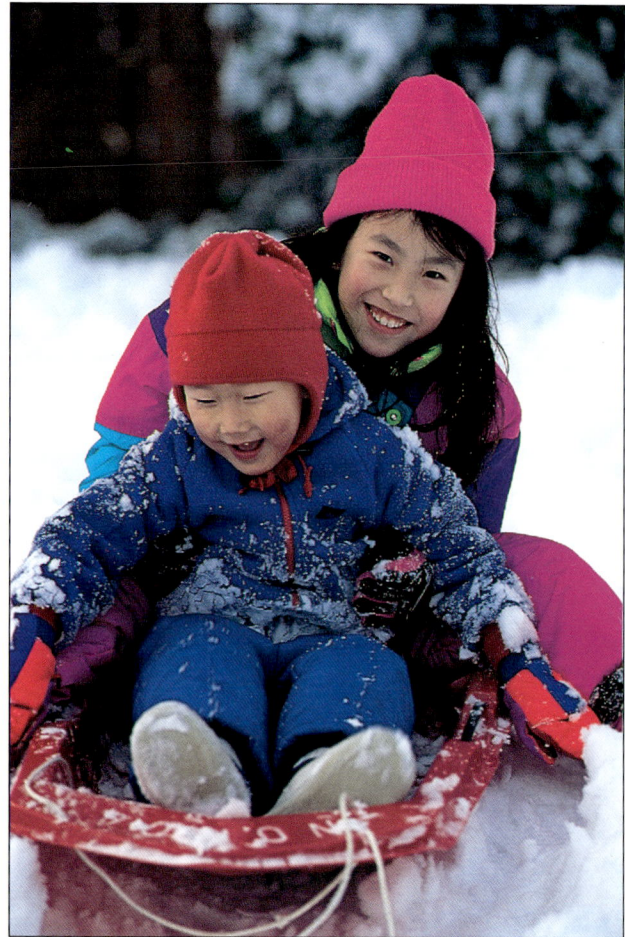

...or tobogganed in the snow? Which kind of weather do you like best?

The water we drink...

...comes from the rain.

The Sun helps wheat to grow...

...and then we can make it into bread.

Animals and weather

Different animals like different kinds of weather.

Mice curl up to sleep all through winter.

This horse has a blanket on to keep warm.

Penguins live in cold, snowy places.

Lizards need the warmth of the Sun.

Frogs like damp, rainy places.

Amazing weather

Sometimes, the weather makes all sorts of amazing things happen.

Hail is frozen rain.

Look out! Here comes a tornado.

What has the fierce
hurricane done?

Rivers can flood when there
is too much rain.

What do
sunshine and
rain make
together?

When would you wear these different clothes?

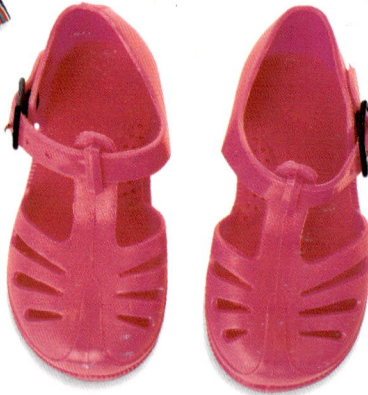